|Ascention|

These are the only two existing photos from that time.

Top: Grafitti in B.C.

Bottom: Kate

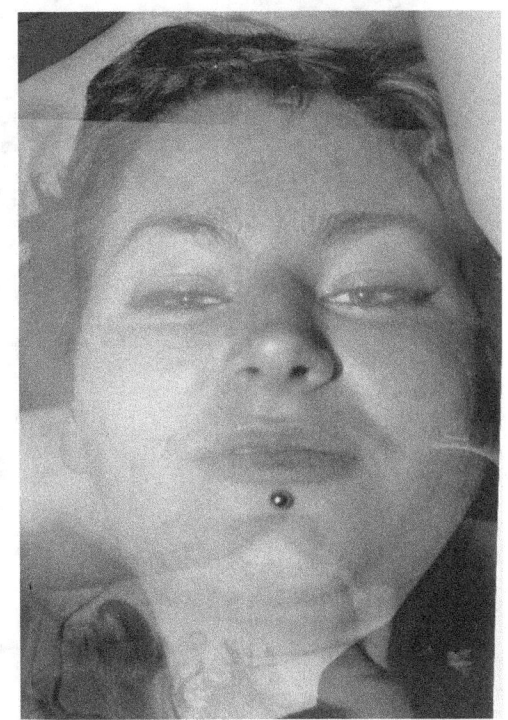

|Goin' Ape| a 55min film by : toly a.k.

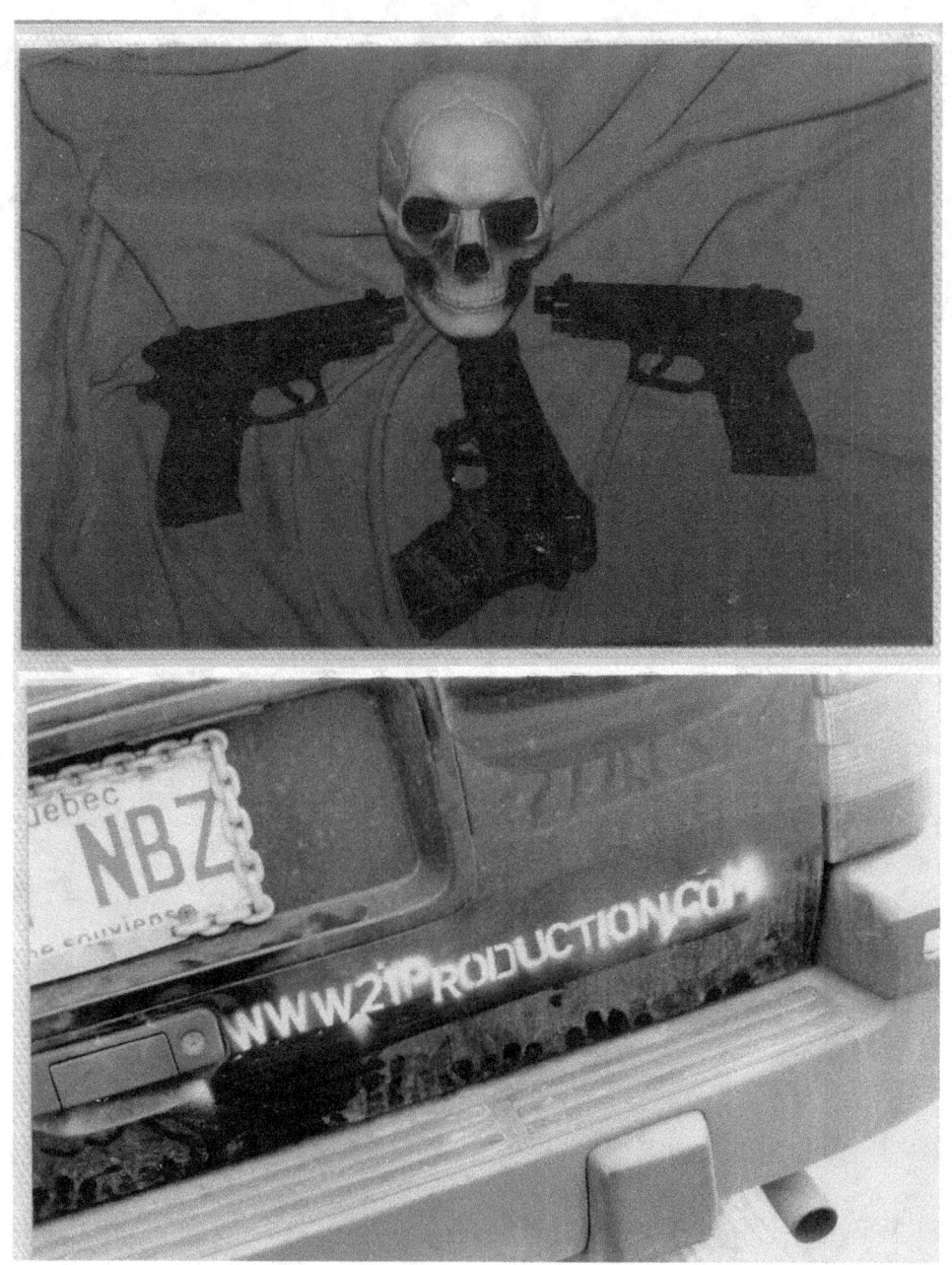

Toly a.k. by the docks Montreal

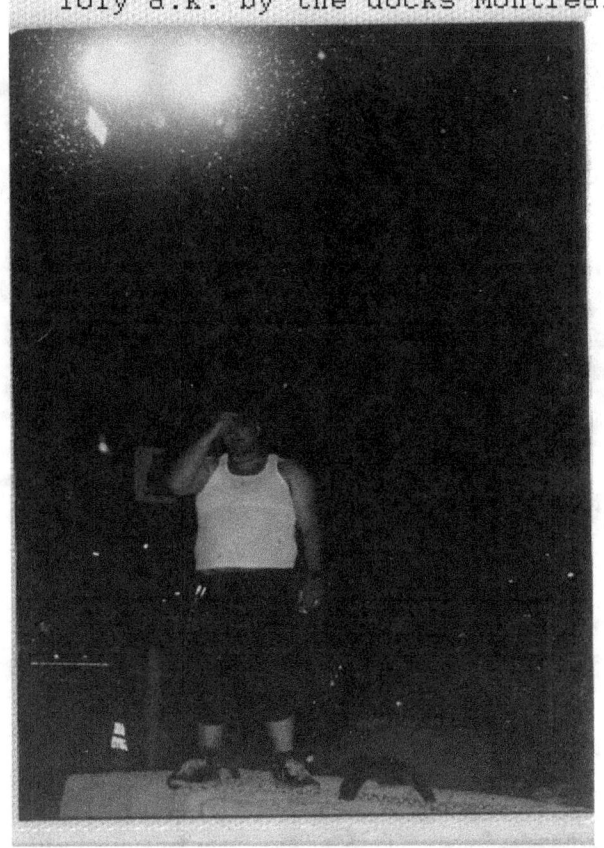

eric heroux   Hosee   Toly a.k.

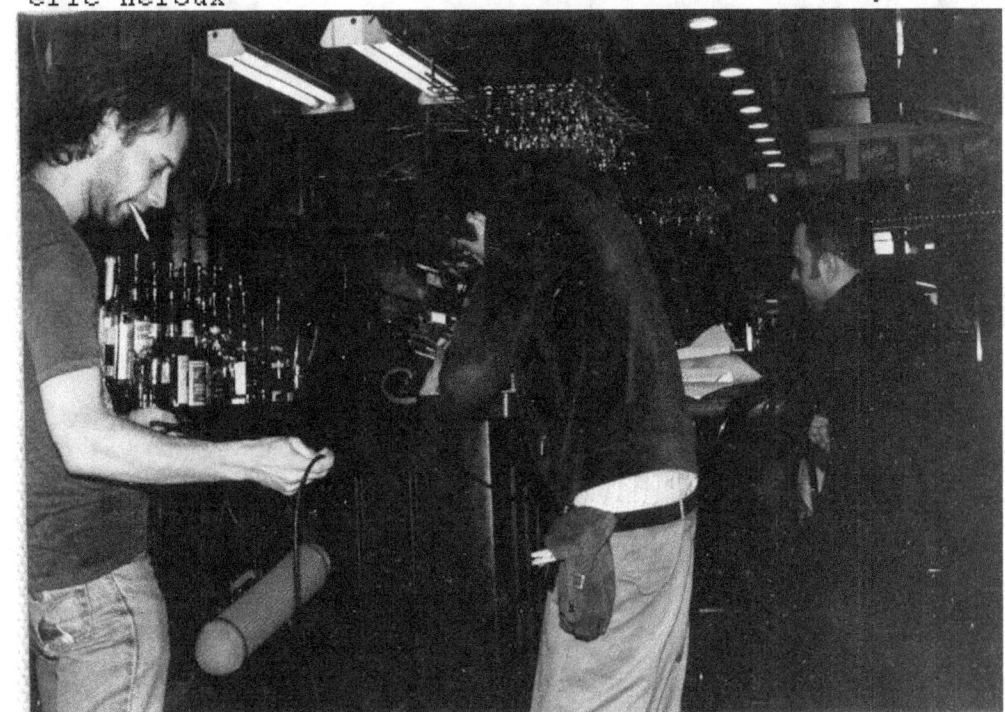

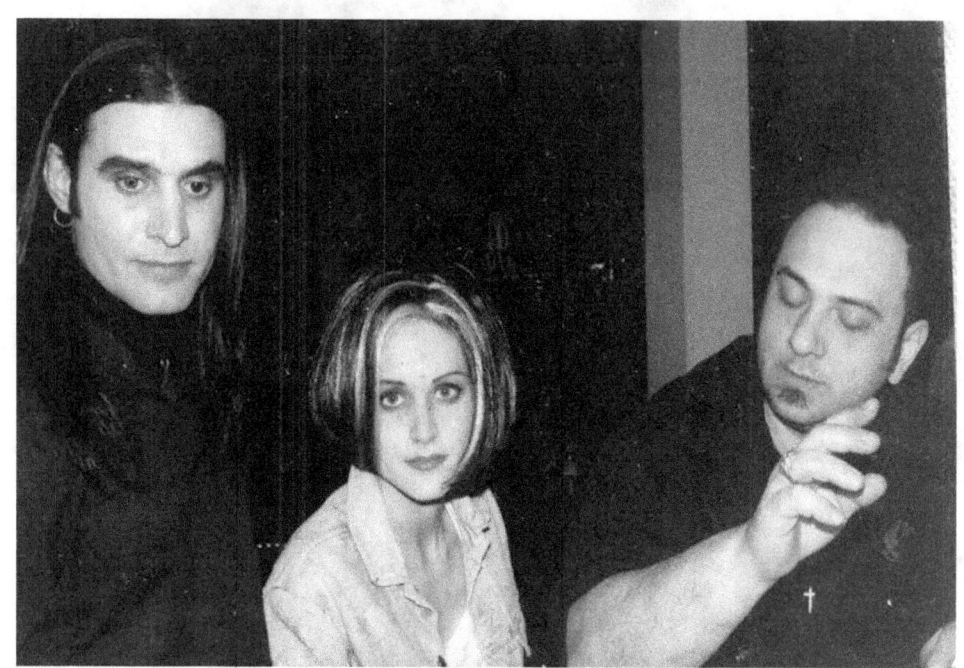

elias varoutsos   Toly A.K. -directing

leela marcelino

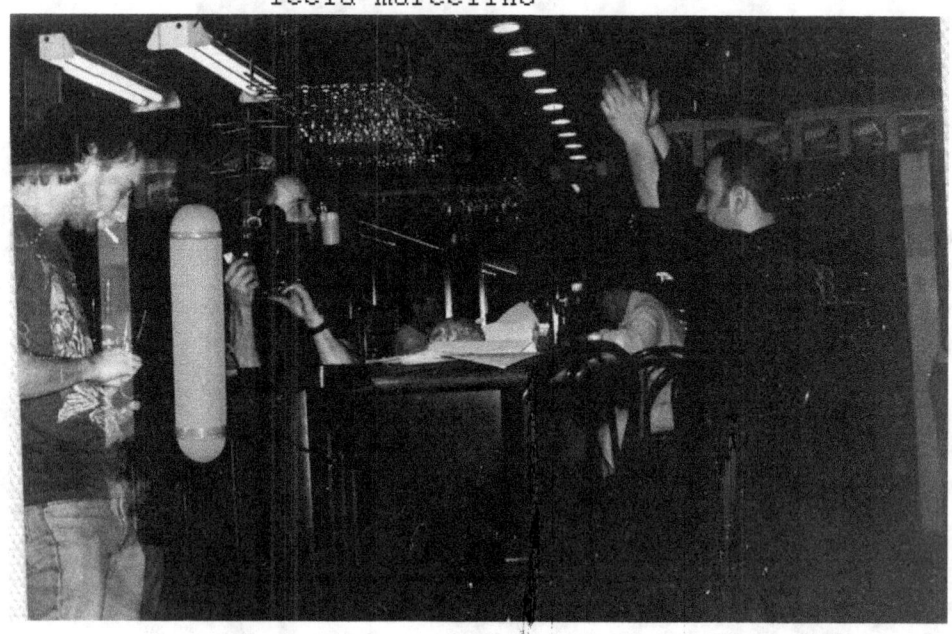

Eric Heroux   Toly a.k. -directing

Michael Wees_d.p.p

Toly a.k.-as ape

on location-verdun qc

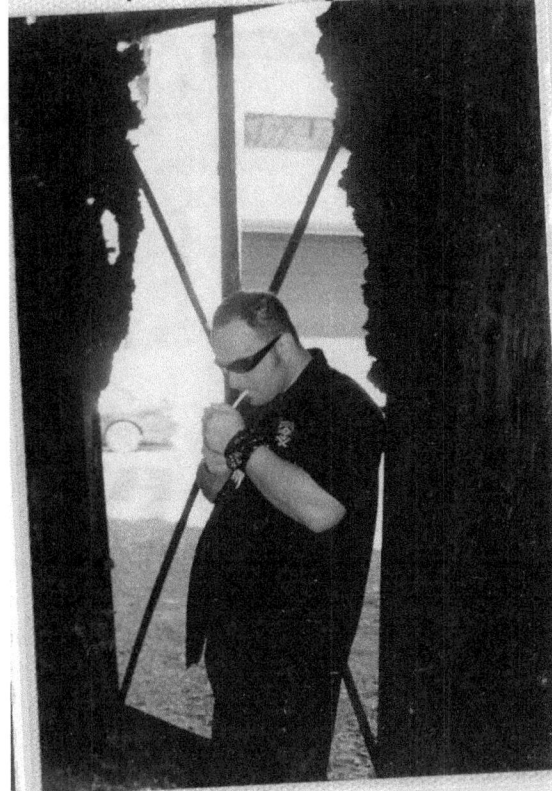

Ryan alman-mario

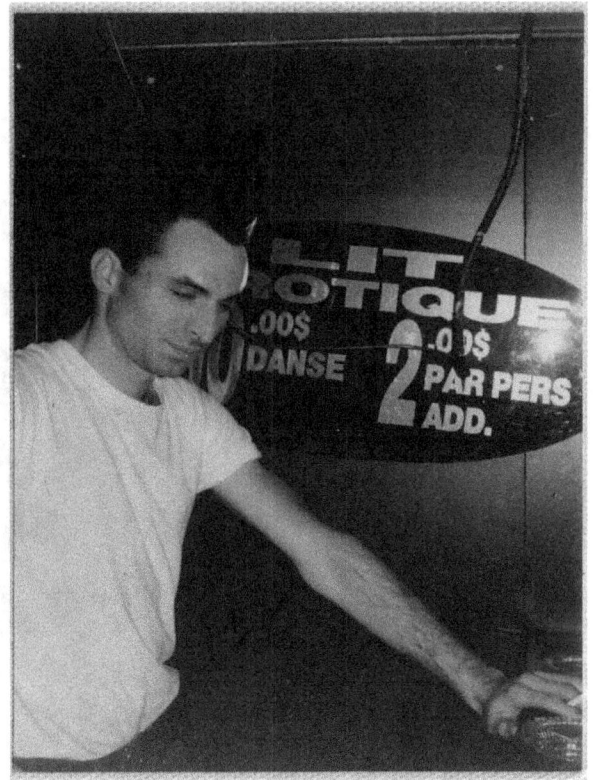

on location-mercier qc
paradise bar

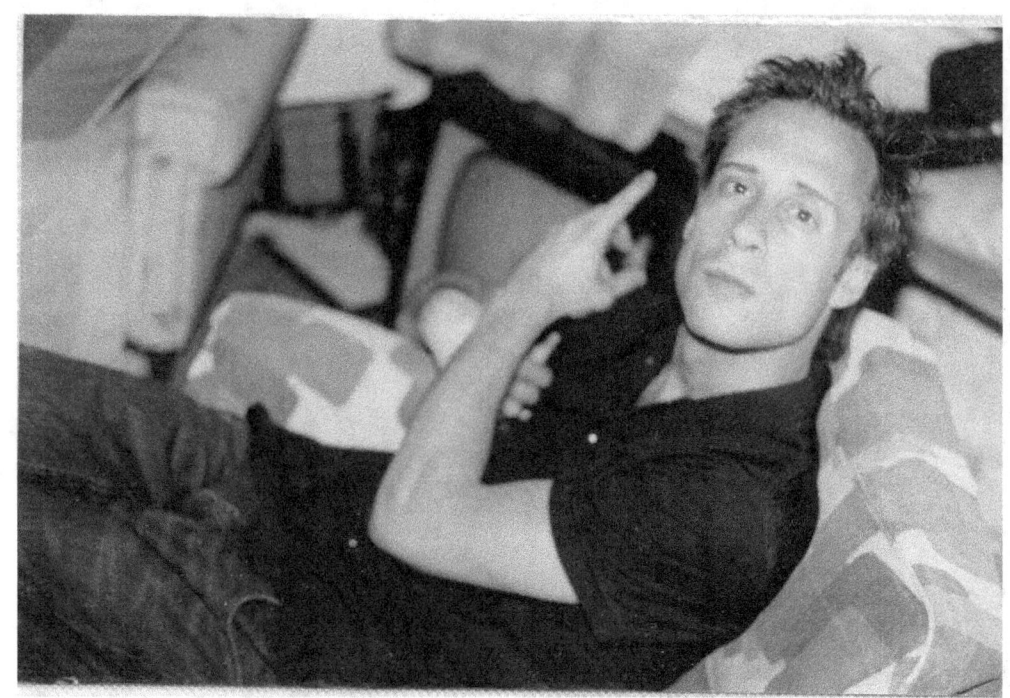

Eric Heroux-as sleeze merchant

Leela marcellino-
as street punk girl

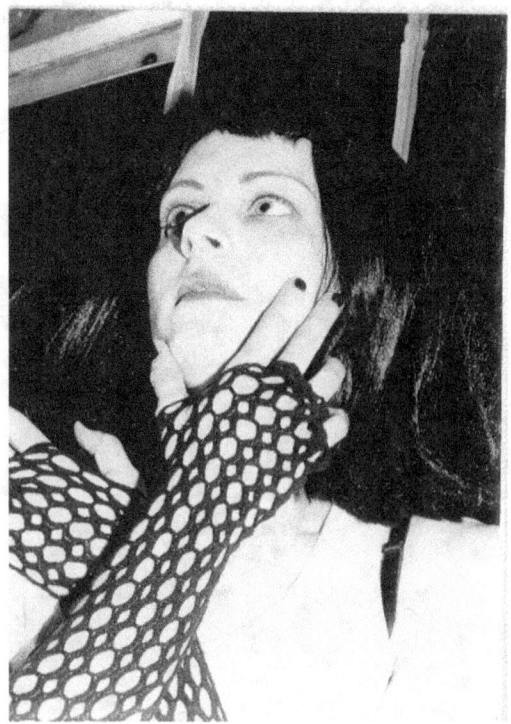

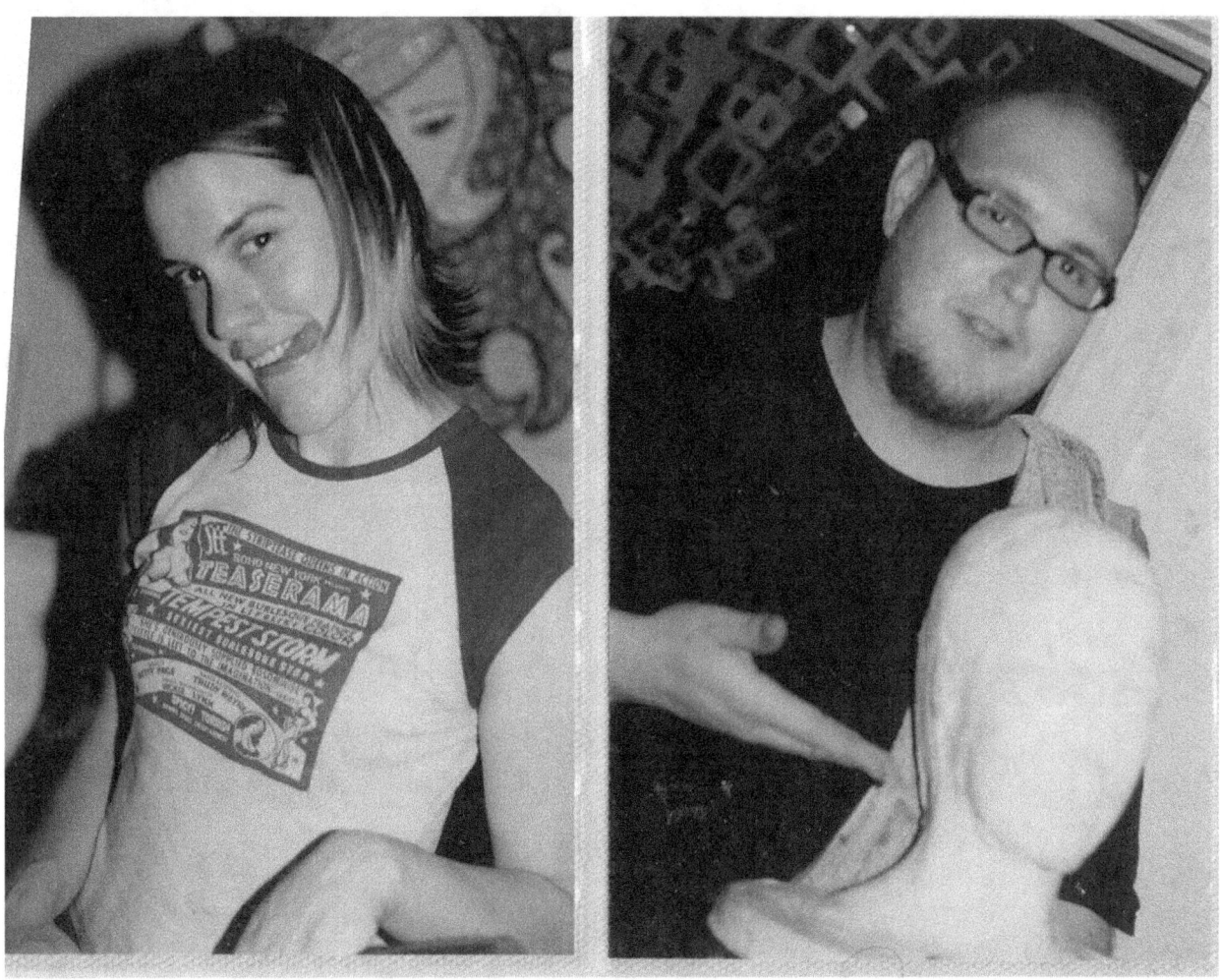

Stephanie weber Biron- D.O.P.

luca Pompillio-fx/make up

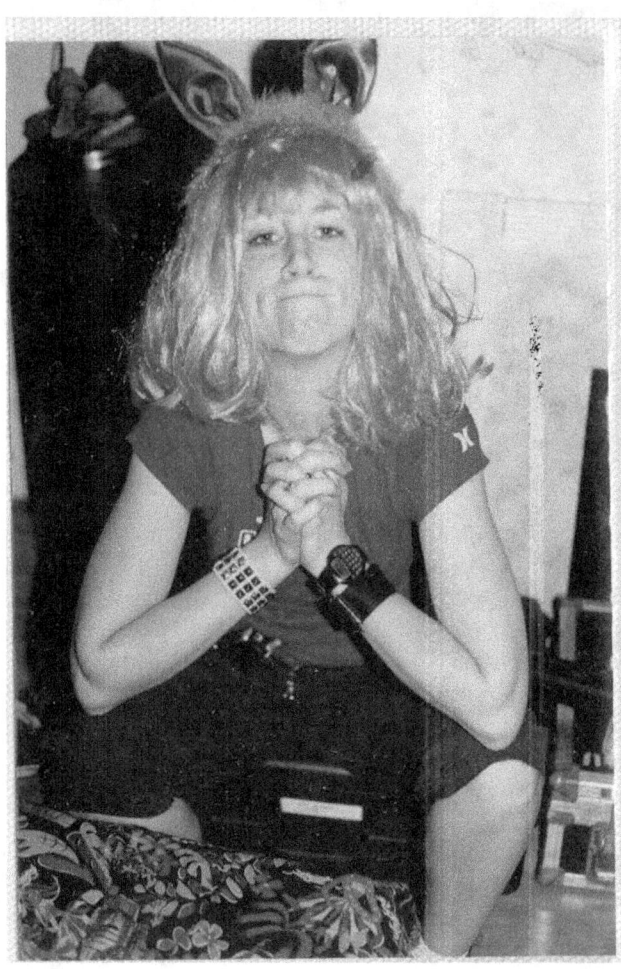

Amanda Ruthman-sound

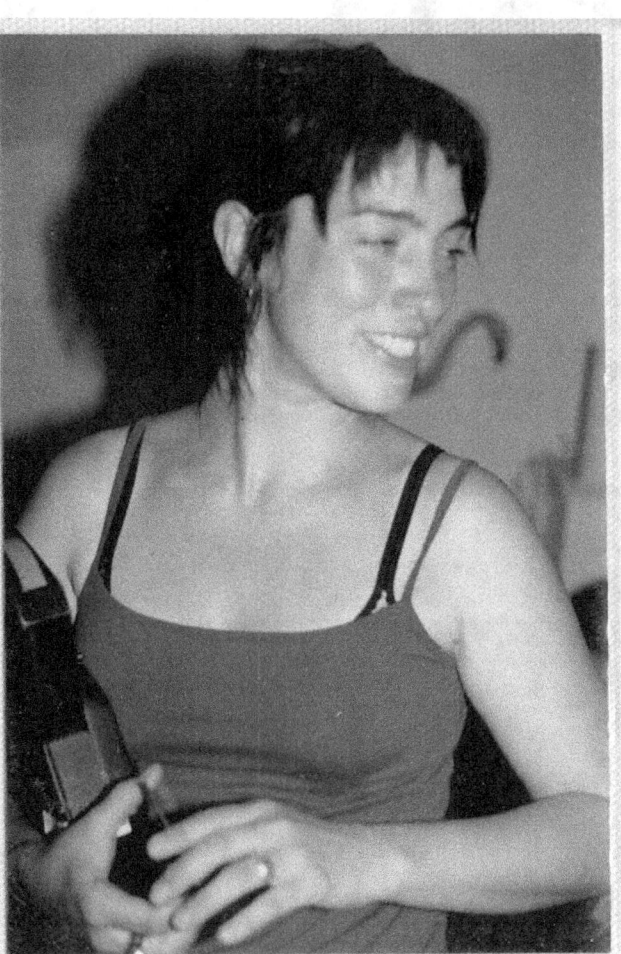

Abeille-camera assist

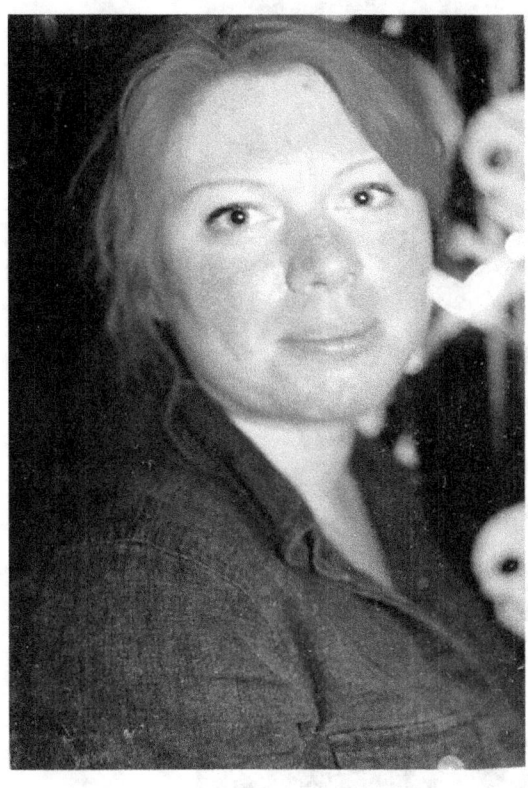

Natasha Clayton

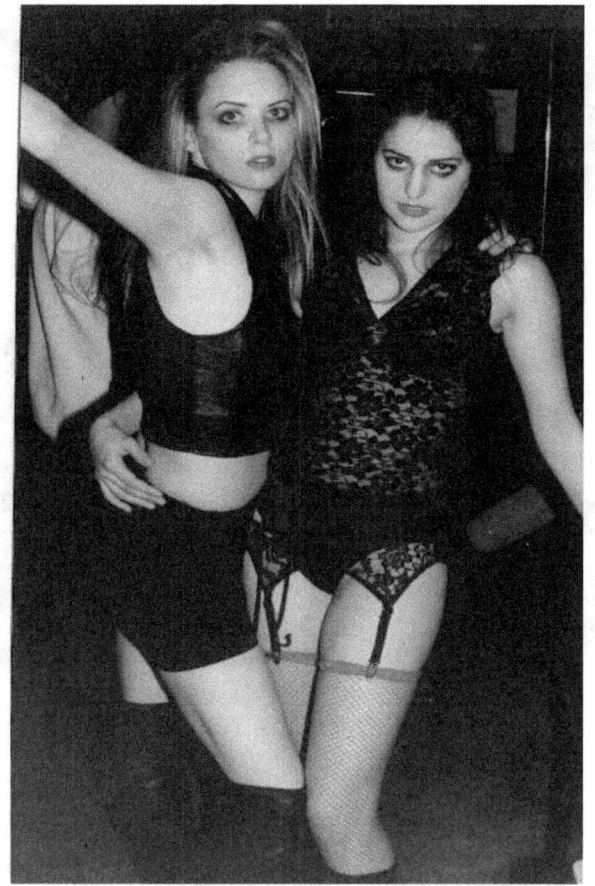

Bianca Jones-strippers-Christine Ghawi

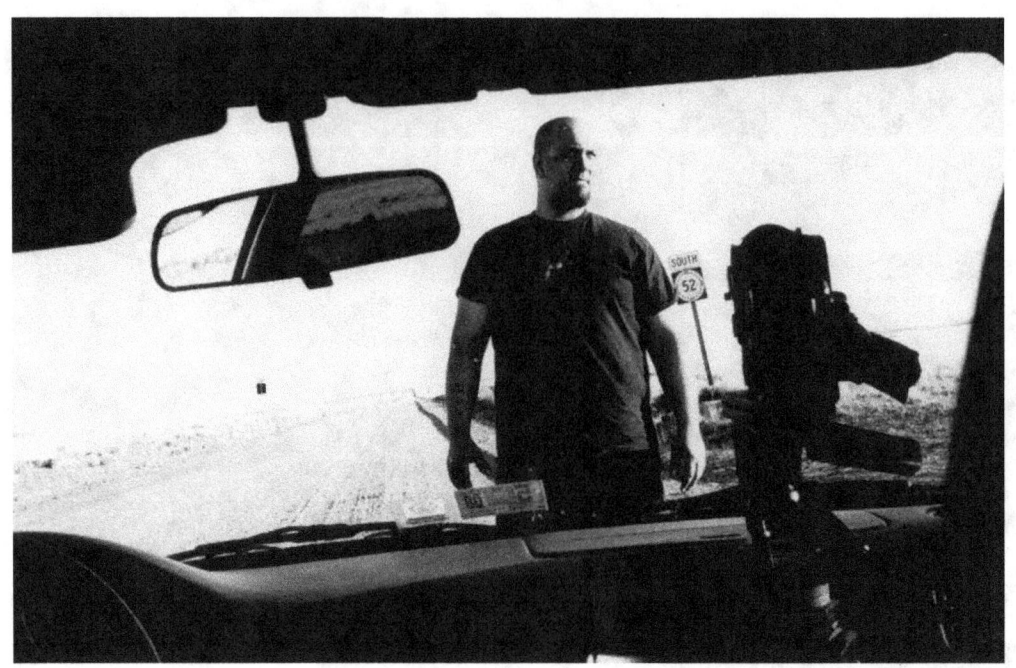

Toly A.K. msking of road movie

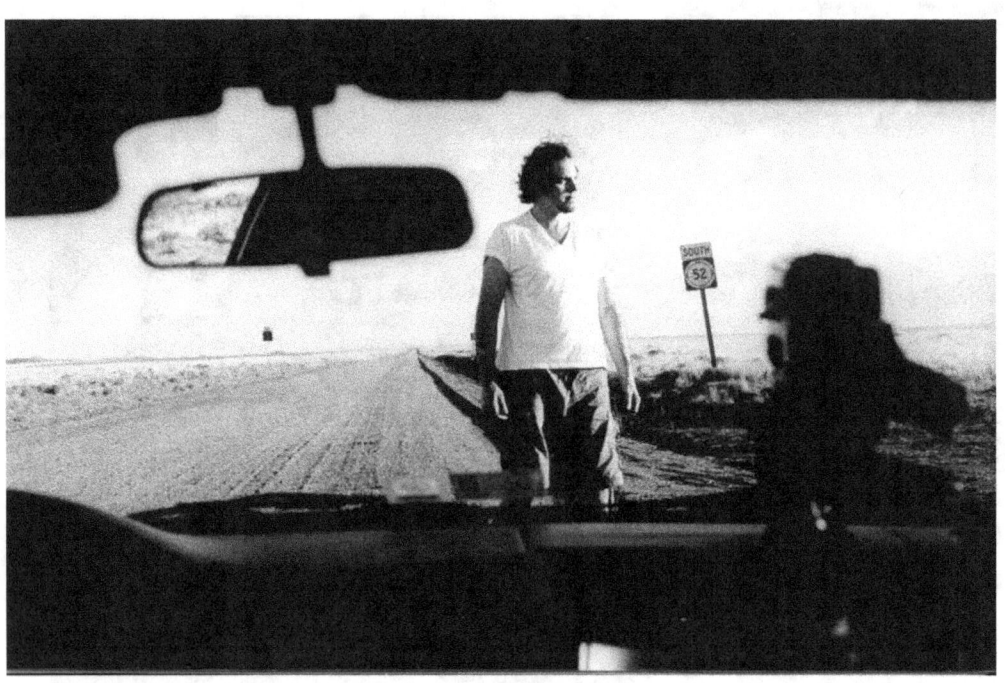

Nicholas E.W.Syracuse-making of road movie

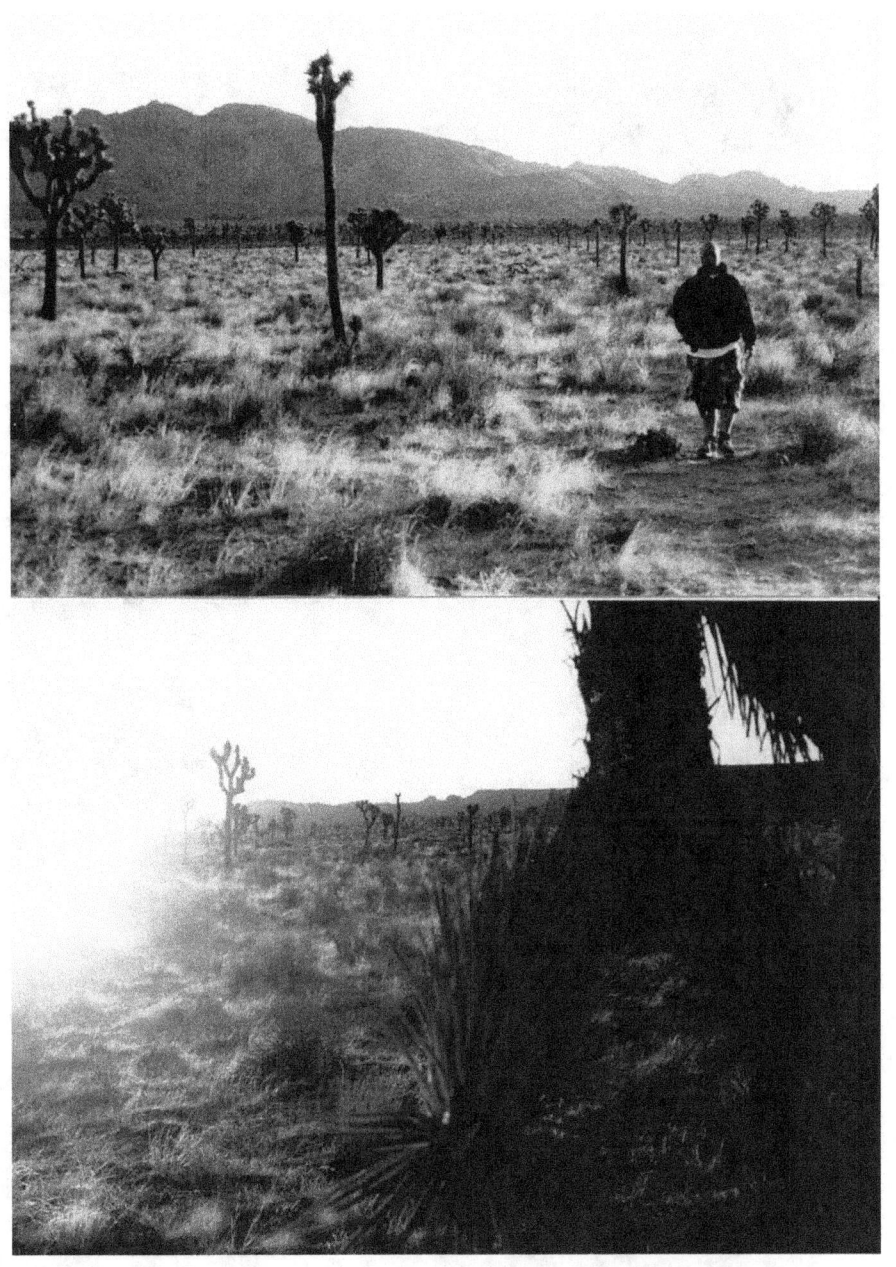

Toly A.K. at Joshua tree

on the road to
Burning man.

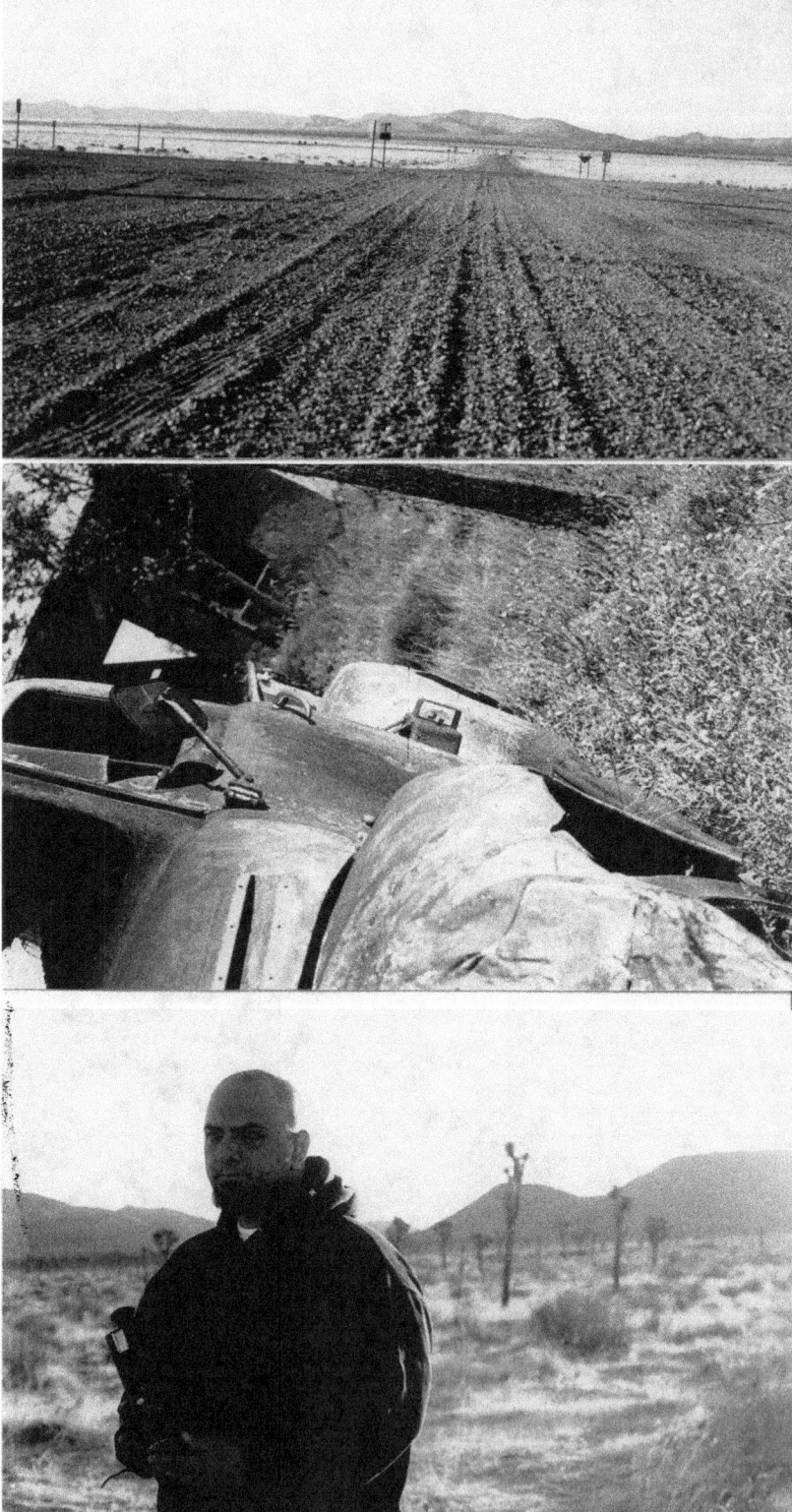

Toly A.k.
with super 8
pixelation camera

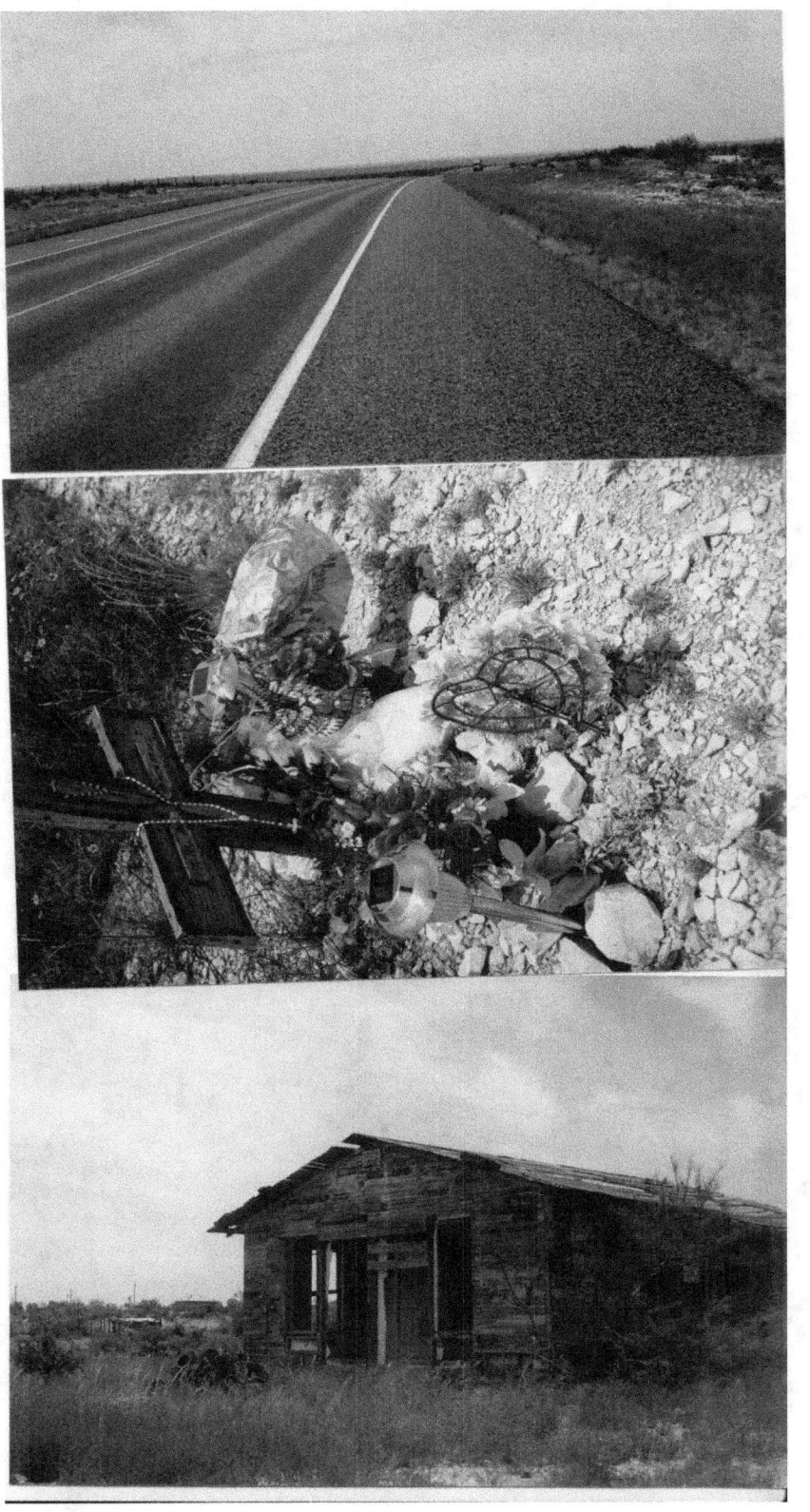

The Road.

On the way to
New Orleans

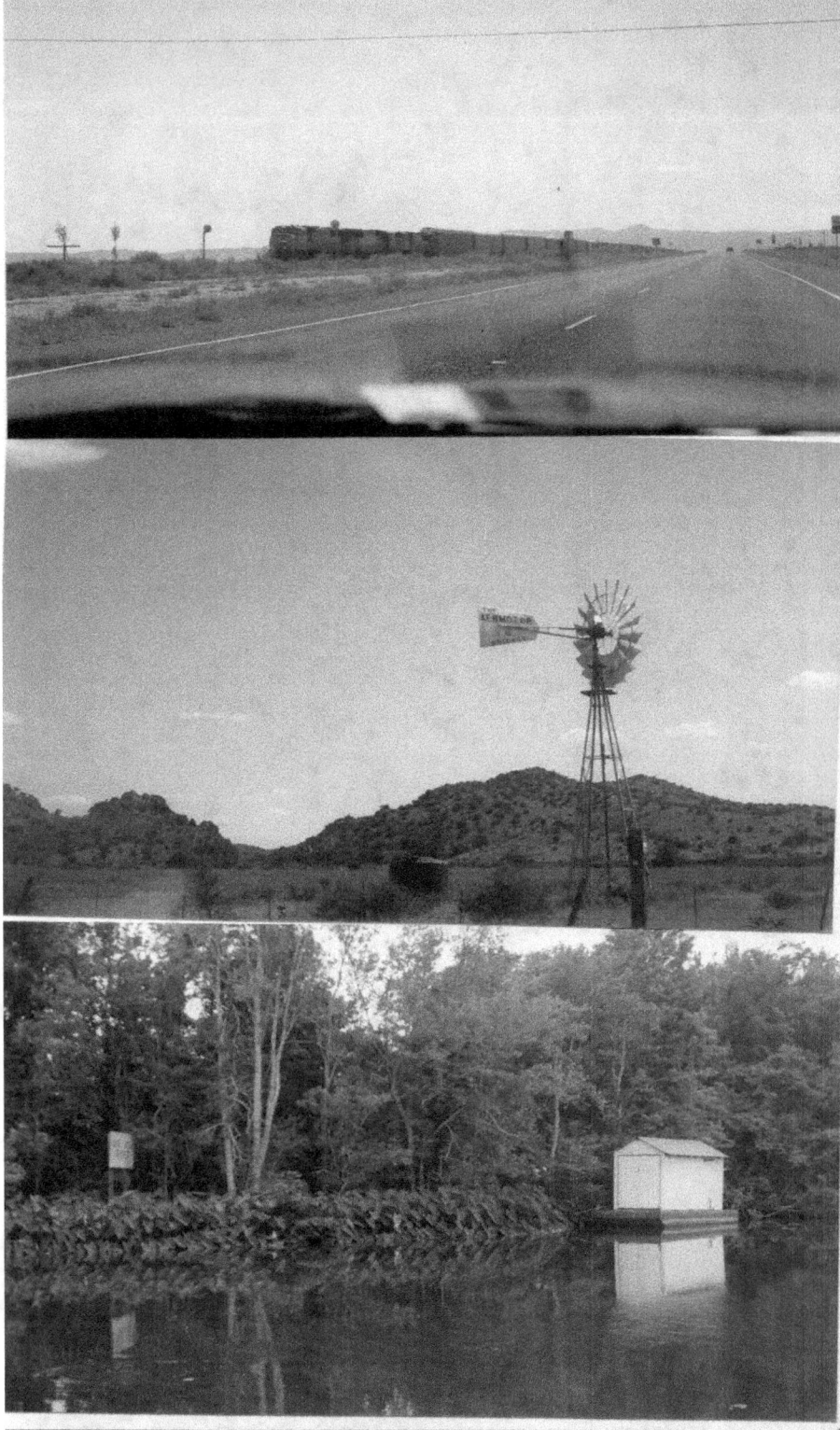

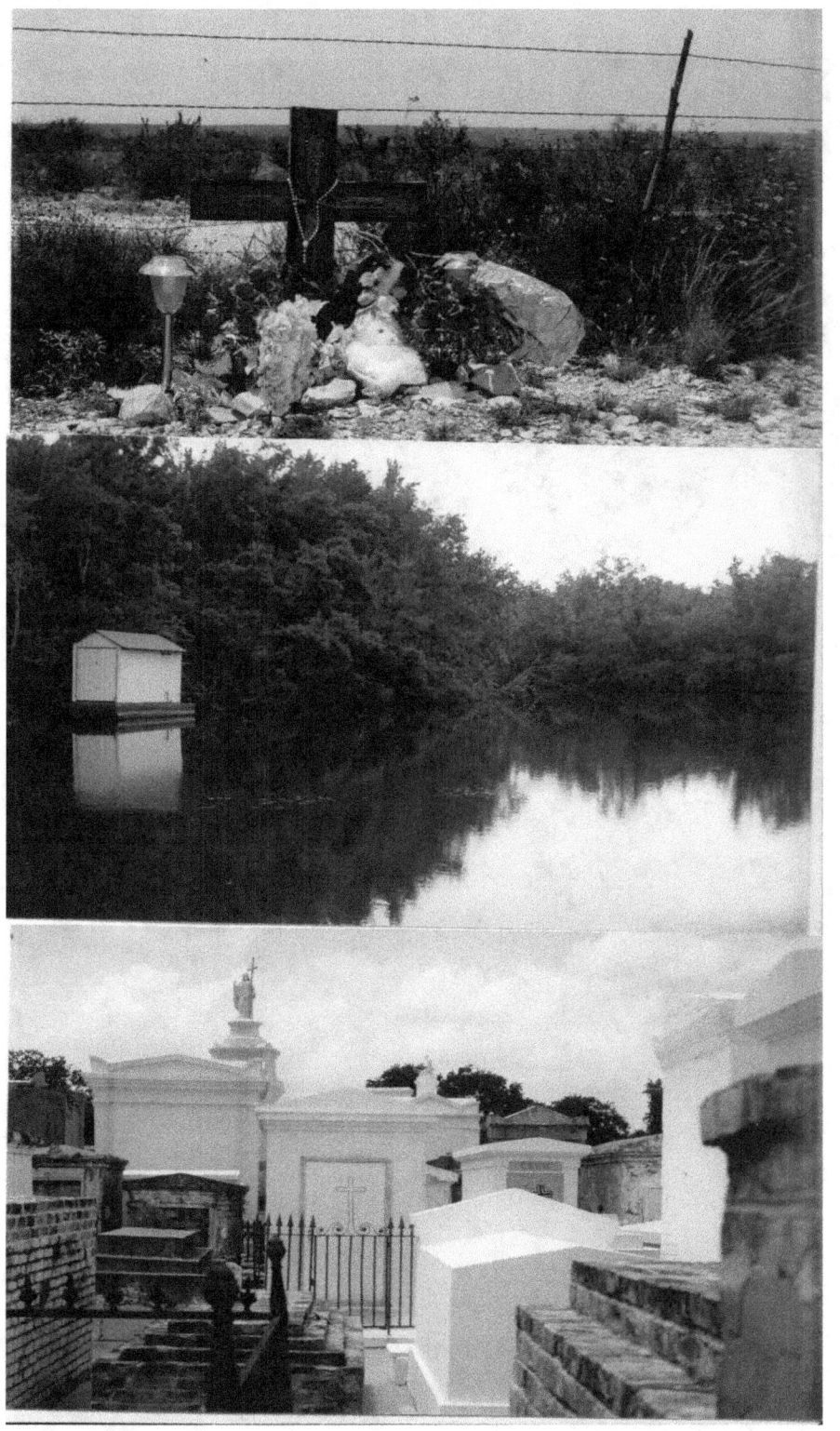

New Orlesns

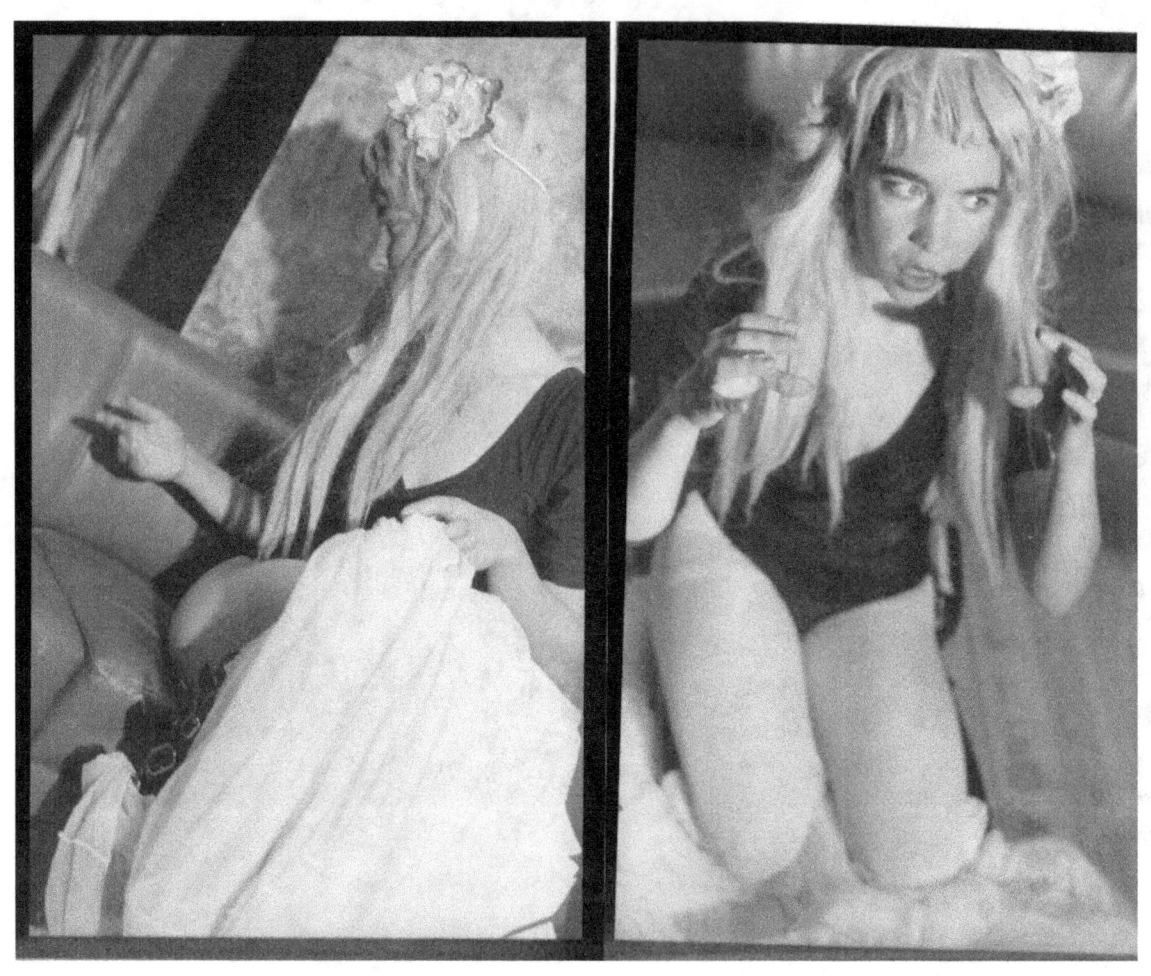

Solstice moon-Griffon Town mtl
kelly elizabeth escofferi

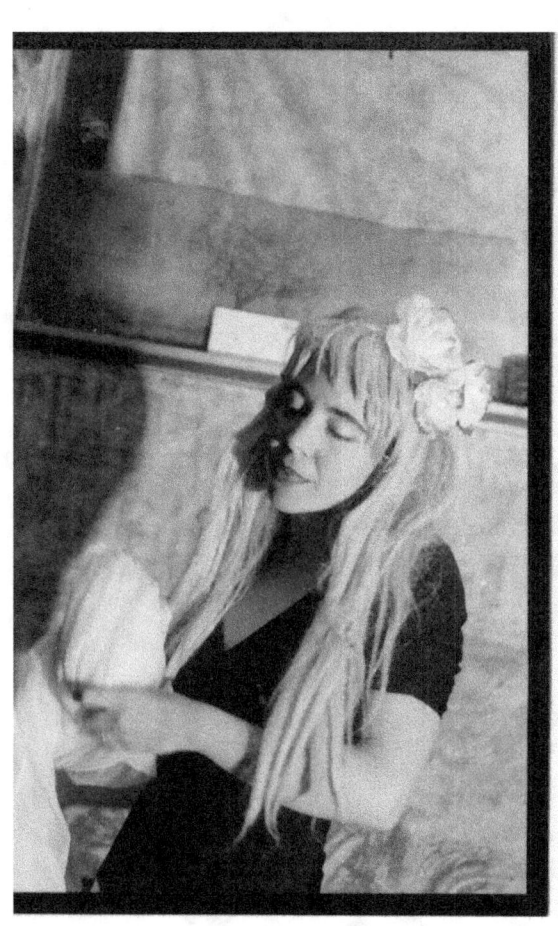
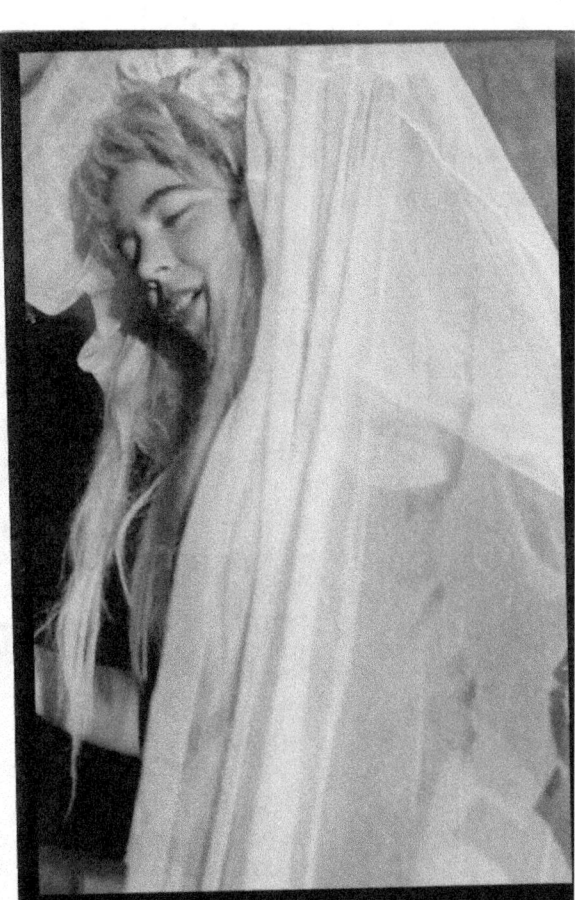

"Reversal of Fortune"
Toly A.K. 2013/14

Exterior: Cemetary, New Orleans. An old woman with dreads lets some old bones slide from her hand onto a stone slab. She begins to chant in an ancient, unearthly voice, not known to scholars.
The lid on the coffinbegins to shake and crack open.
A zombie arises.
She beckons to him to do her bidding.

Title card: The pretty people.

Exterior: Log cabin. Lucy and Mark are packing their S.U.V.

    Lucy
This place gave me the creeps , mark.

    Mark
They're coming for you, Barbara!

    Lucy
They might be.

    Mark
Listen Lucy, theirs nothing
out here except swamp rats and
gators. I don't mind shoving off
early but have a sense of humour
about it would ya?

    Lucy
Where did you find it? It. it.com?

    Mark
Go fuck yourself, stay home and
watch American television and radio!

    Lucy
Ok - gladiator-mr. Canada speaks!

    Mark
Fuckin American.

    Lucy
Fuck you, mark, that a.t.c. looks mighty
your driveway along with your
snowmobile. All that hockey equipment
    Lucy(con't)
must have been pretty expensive. That's

a nice pair of skates and hummer. Tell
me how did you afford to gas all that,
and bring me to this expensive cabin
in the woods?

      Mark
Fuck, Lucy. Fine.

      Lucy
Credit card maxed, maybe?

      Mark
I'm taking you home.

      Lucy
Better gas up!

      Mark
Oh, we'll gas up.

      Lucy
Its been a gas.

      Mark
Whats that?

      Lucy
Gassed im sure.

Exterior: The Hummer navigates through a thicket of brusgh, they come across a gas station. A gas attendant exits.

      Gas attendant
How much?

      Mark(getting out)
20 bucks.
I was expecting to see more
black people out here.

      Gas attendant
Huh?

      Mark
You know like in Family guy?
      Gas attendant
The south isn't that way anymore.

      Mark

We love the south in Canada

  Gas attendeant
What now?

  Mark
Here's the 20 bucks

  Gas attendeant
Is it trie what they say?

  Mark
What?

  Gas attendeant
That you don't lock your doors, aren't you afraid of the black people...tssst racist.

  Mark
Small town...

  Gas attendeant
Yep.
(puts the 20 bucks in his shirt.
Better make like a banana
and split.

  Lucy
Mark, what did you say?

  Mark
Nothing the guys an a-hole.

  Lucy
Colourful use of metaphor as always.

Fromthe distance, on a hill top, a man is slowly moving-at a slow gate.

Interior: Hummer.

  Lucy
How did you pay for your Hummer?

  Mark
I work for a broadcaster.

          Lucy
Its Canada broadcasters don't make money

          Mark
We're on the take. Cigarettes, casinos, cocaine. Journalists plug police reports to run interference with people and the cops. White noise.

          Lucy
Tricky

          Mark
its all run from prison, for the most part. There is no real thing as freedom anymore, life on the outside is a thick set of rules.

          Lucy
Stop the car

          Mark
Okay.

They walk and sit by the rivers edge.

          Lucy
Why are you telling this?

          Mark
Because youre a bitch i could trust you.

          Lucy
I cant stand your guts right now.

          Mark
But youre still here
(take out a smoke)
          Got a light?
(she lights ity for him)
          See... bitch!

          Lucy(laughingly)
Fuck you, man!

          Lucy
I knew we made the mob, by being narrow minded toward

                    immigrants in the 20's,
                    but on the take?
                         Mark
                    What do YOU mean made the mob?

                         Lucy
                    Well, some mobs or gangs.

                         Mark(laughs)
                    oh, you mean how we get immigrant
                    sons criminal records, dumb ones
                    and then make fun of them when
                    theyre not around?

                         Lucy
                    Yeah.

                         Mark
                    Thats the shit!

                         Lucy
                    No mark, thats sucks. A day of
                    judgement is coming.

                         Mark
                    Thats some cryptic shit!
He leans over to kiss her, she reaches for his crotch, but he's
flaccid.

                         Lucy
                    What is it, is it me?

He shoves her off him.

                         Lucy
                    Fuckin asshole!

                         Mark
                    Bitch!
She storms off.

                         Lucy
                    Fuckin cock smoker!

She hears a low moan through a ticket of brush. She stops dead in her
tracks and pears through and sees an albino zombie with one arm. She
screams but he's on top of her. He bites her arm. She pulls her arm
away as a chunk of flesh comes off and runs into the distance.

Exterior: mausoleum. The crypt door rests open. projected on top are the souls of dead slaves burned on crosses.
The voodoo queen exits from the crypt and raises her arms chanting. Zombies rise from their grave.

Title card: "trouble in the hood"

Interior: Mr. Tibbs is sitting in a small apartment on his bed, playing a blues melody on his guitar. He sets the guitar down and turns on the t.v. a roideao clown jumps over a fence, out the way of a bull.

          Mr. Tibbs.
Tsk.

A journalist comes on the tube.

          Journalist
Beat him up.

          Mr tibbs
Beat who up?
Whats with this station?

          Journalist
Don't let him make it.

          Mr. Tibbs
Which brother are thses white
honkys making trouble for in
the hood now?

Cindy curvy girl wlaks into the room

          Cindy
you talking to me?

          Mr. Tibbs
The culture clash in this country
keeps on shocking me

          Cindy
Your names not really mr. Tibbs is it?

          Mr tibbs
Yes, cindy it is, why?

                    Cindy
          Nevermind

                Mr tibbs
          So thats it huh?

                 Cindy
          You know you and i aint cut
          out for the real world.

                Mr tibbs
          Whats real? You walk out that door,
          don't look back.

                  Cindy(putting her dress on)
          I'll just put on my Freudian slip!
          goodbye, mr tibbs.You know im
          only faithful for four hours.

Cindy walks out of the door. It shuts behind her. Mr tibbs take out
an old beat up guitar case and loads the guitar into it.

Exterior: mr tibbs opens the door to a rusty '57 chevyand puts the
guitar in the back seat-gets in he drivers seat and drives off.

                    Mr Tibbs
              Yes Cindy, It is, Why?

                    Cindy
              (smirking)Nevermind.

                    Mr Tibbs
              So that's it, huh?

                    Cindy
          You know you and I ain't cut out for the real world.

                    Mr. Tibbs
          What's real, anyway? You walk out that door, don't look back.

                    Cindy
               (putting her dress on)
          I'll just put on my Freudian slip. Goodbye, Mr. Tibbs.

Cindy walks out the door. It shuts behind her. Mr. Tibbs takes out a beat up guitar case and loads a guitar into it.

Exterior: Mr. Tibbs opens the door to rusty '57 Chevy and puts the guitar in the backseat, gets in the driver-seat and drives off.

Interior: Peter, a con who kills his socio-self(suicidal serial killer). He is a dark, Mediterranean type. He walks into his parents' kitchen. His mother, an old woman, is by the stove.

                      Peter
        Ma, where are my old pictures of my ex-wife?

                      Mom
        I don't know what you are talking about.

                      Peter
        You burned them, didn't you?

She doesn't answer. Peter walks down the staircase into the basement and lies down.

                      Peter
        Man, this sucks.

Peter stares into the mirror, backlit by a light on the nightstand. He stares into his silhouette and places a hat on his head. He opens a drawer in the 19th century chest of drawers in front of his and takes out a knife with a serrated edge. Light dances off the edge of the blade.

                      Mom(O.S.)
        Peter, what are you doing?

Peter looks up to the top of the stairs which divide them.

                      Peter
        Going out.

Exterior: Dirt road.
Mark is driving recklessly across the underbrush

                      Mark
        Lucy! I can't leave her out here.

He stops and tries his cellphone

                      Mark

                         No reception!

He puts the truck in gear as Lucy comes out from behind a tree and
falls onto the hood of the truck.

                              Mark
                         Lucy, shit!

Mark gets out of the truck and stoops down to pick Lucy up.

                              Mark
                         Are you alright?

Lucy's eyes are rolled back into her head.

                            Mark(con't)
                         Shit!

He slaps her.

                              Lucy
                         What the fuck?

                              Mark
                         Ok, good.

Mark sees her arm

                            Mark(con't)
                         What's with you arm?

                              Lucy
                         If I told you, you wouldn't believe me.

                              Mark
                         I have a first aid kit, hold on.

Exterior: Back of hummer, Lucy and Mark are sitting on the ground.
Her wound is dressed.

                              Mark
                         I think you've lost your marbles.

                              Lucy
                         Don't say it, huh?

                              Mark
                         C'mon, we're going into town.

Exterior: deserted town.

>						Mark
> What's with this town?

>						Lucy
> Where is everyone?

>						Mark
> There's a diner. I see someone inside, let's check it out.

Interior: Diner. Cindy is sitting in front of a plate of meat, cooked rare. Mark and Lucy enter. A bell above the door rings but Cindy doesn't turn around. Mark looks at Lucy, baffled, turns and walks to Cindy.

>						Mark
> Hey lady, where is everyone?

>						Cindy
> Busy, I guess. It's still early.

Cindy cuts a piece of meat from the slab in front of her as Mark looks on, and takes a big bite, licking her lips.

>						Cindy(con't)
> Want some breakfast?

>						Mark
> I think we'll pass.

Cindy takes a last bite, gets up and walks behind the counter. From underneath the counter an zombie head is seen. With chopped up pieces of flesh.

Cindy walks over and sees Lucy's arm.

>						Cindy
> Dog bite?

>						Lucy
> Uh, yeah.

>						Cindy
> Must have stung

>						Lucy
> You could say that.

                        Cindy
                  I could say a lot.

                        Mark
          You two going to go at it like the cat and the canary?

                        Cindy
                  I dont bite. Unless I'm hungry.

tares at her blankly.

or: Mr. Tibbs is pushing his old Chevy into the parking lot. He
to a stop, takes out his guitar and strums a chord leaving in
r. Mark walks out of the diner shoving the door open with a

                        Mark
                How come the town folk aren't around?

                        Mr. Tibbs
ng, I guess. It's dawn. See the morning sun is just coming over
                        that ridge.

ooks over at the ridge squinting. It the distance, he sees a
 moving slowly.
                        Mark
                Hey, there's someone! Hey, over here!

ooks on in horror.

                        Lucy
                  Mark, that's no person.

                        Mark
            What? Don't start with that zombie bullshit again.

bs laughs.

                        Mr. Tibbs
s! Why, I've heard a lot of things but a real live, or should i
                    say dead-zombie!

                        Cindy
                        Undead

                        Mr. Tibbs
                Look at you all dolled up.

        Cindy
    Got all dolled up for you, too.

        Mr. Tibbs
     Come away with me then.

        Cindy
   That jalopy ain't goin' no place.

        Mark
 My truck is runnin'. We're leaving; two bit town.

        Lucy
       Mark...

        Mark
       What?

        Lucy
       Mark...

        Mark
       What?!

Mark wheels around on his heels to see a zombie behind him.

        Mark
      What the fuck?

        Lucy
       Hit it!

Mark punches the zombie in the face. It stops in its tracks, then gives Mark an evil stare and lunges at him. A man, Peter, brushes past Mark from behind knocking him and the zombie off their feet. Peter drives a serrated knife into the head of the zombie.

        Mark
   No, it can't be, but it is.

Peter adjusts his hat. Mr. Tibbs walks over and pushes the zombie with his foot.

        Mr. Tibbs
It's dead. You know what I mean. Lucky you came prepared.

        Mark
      Yeah, Lucky.

Peter
Name's Pete

Mark
I think I'll keep calling you Lucky.

Peter
As you wish. Hey Cindy have you two eaten?

Cindy
Nope.

Peter
I suggest you eat some grub.

Interior: Diner.

Mark
Think there's more of them out there, like that one and the one that bit Lucy?

Mr. Tibbs
Don't know. Maybe. Just passing through actually. I see that thing out there didn't spoil your appetite Mark.

Mark
Nope. How about you, Lucky?

Lucky(Peter) is distant. Lucy puts her hand on his shoulder. Lucky looks up, there's a tear in his eye.

Lucy
Peter, you okay?

Peter
Can I talk to you a minute?

Interior: Diner. Lucy and Peter are sitting at a table.

Lucy
What's wrong?

Peter
It was only a month ago that she left me.

Lucy
Who?

                    Peter
        My betrothed. She left me standing at the alter.

                    Lucy
              That must hurt.

                    Mark
            Felt like an altar boy.

                    Lucy
            You're no altar boy.

They stare into each others' eyes as if they were about to kiss. Lucy breaks their stare.

                    Mark
             Lucy? Hey, hey Lucy?
             We gotta hit the road.

                    Lucy
              Guess we gotta.

Exterior: A squad car pulls up. A cop exits.

Interior: Diner

                    Peter
              The boys in blue.

                    Mark
                    Great.

Mark opens the diner door.

                  Mark(con't)
         Hey, in here! Now we can get some answers.

Interior: Cop 1 enters the diner.

                    Mark
What's with this town? That thing comes out of nowhere and the whole
                 town's deserted.

                    Cop 1
                What thing?

Mark looks out the window. Cop 2 is standing in the spot the zombie was in.

                              Mark
                              Shit!

                              Cop 1
What thing? The town's folk are spooked enough without you runnin' at
                           the mouth.

                              Mark
                             Spooked?

                              Cop 1
        Haven't you heard there's a killer on the loose?

                              Lucy
                   Zombies and a serial killer.

                              Cop 1
              What kind of drugs is you kids on?

                              Mark
                          Drugs? I wish.

                              Cop 1
             We can figure it out at the station house.

                              Mark
                         This is bullshit.

                              Cop 1
       Keep your mouth shut or I'll bust you for resisting arrest.

Interior: Small town, jail cell. The boys and the girls are locked up
behind bars in the same makeshift cell.

                              Cindy
         I've never been in here before. Plenty of dungeons. I thought it
                          would be bigger.

                              Peter
                     We can order room service.

                              Mark
                             Good one.

                            Mr. Tibbs
           Shoot, they even have us all in here together.

Cindy

Like we're going to cuddle.

                Mr. Tibbs
That's not what you said the other night

                Cindy
That's exactly what I said.

                Mr. Tibbs
What did I say?

                Cindy
Get out or.

                Mr. Tibbs
I doubt it.

                Cindy
Charmed, I'm sure.

                Lucy
We gotta get outta here.

                Mark
Let's put our heads together. Maybe there's a way out.

                Cop 1
           (banging on the bars)
Sleep it off. I'll let you out in the morning.

                Lucy
The morning. By that time the whole town will be zombies.

                Cop 2
Always carry around a knife like this?

                Peter
Just during duck season.

                Cop 2
Ain't no ducks around here, boy.

                Peter
You gonna lock me up?

                Cop 2
With pleasure.

Cop 2 opens the cage and throws peter in. Peter snatches the key from the desk as he pushes him in.

Interior: Jail. The cops are asleep. Lucy is sweating and moaning.

> Peter
> Keep her quiet, i don't want the cops to wake up. What's wrong with her?

> Mark
> Don't know. Maybe we can take her to the doctor.

> Cindy
> No doctor can cure what she's got.

> Mr. Tibbs
> Quiet down,

He strokes Lucy's hair. Peter unlatches the cage.

> Peter
> Got it!

> Mark
> Lucky does it again!

> Peter
> Stop calling me lucky.

> Mr. Tibbs
> We ain't out of the woods yet, c'mon.

> Cindy
> She's turning.

> Mark
> (harsh whisper)
> You shut your trap!

The group sneaks past the sleeping cops, down a narrow passageway, and gather at the front door.

> Mr. Tibbs
> Now keep it down.

> Cindy
> About those town folk...

> Mr. Tibbs
> Now now Cindy.

Mr. Tibbs opens the door. The indoor lights light the night sky. Mr Tibbs is horrified by what he sees- the townsfolk dressed in their daily clothing-the butcher-the maid-the mayor- all zombies.

> Mr. Tibbs
> This can't be real.

He backs into the room as a zombie climbs the porch stairs.

> Mark
> Shut the door.

Tibbs looks on.

> Mark
> Tibbs, shut the door.

Mark slams the door shut, chopping off a zombie's fingers as it reaches in. A zombie crashes through the window pulling at Tibbs.

> Mark
> Tibbs!

Mark tries to pull the zombie off Tibbs to no avail. Peter chops the arms off the zombie, hacking at them with a couple gory whacks of his knife.

> Mark
> Got your knife back?

> Peter
> Yep.

Cop 1 and cop 2 come bounding around the corner. Cop 2 sees the zombie and fumbles with the gun in his holster, firing off a round and shooting himself in the foot. The zombie licks at the blood.

> Cop 1
> You bumbling idiot! You, help me prop this table against the window.

> Peter
> But the zombie's in the room.

Cop 1 throws a jacket over the zombie's head as it gets up. The zombie fumbles with the jacket with black ooze spitting out of its arms. The ooze squirting in their faces, Cindy licks her lips.

                    Cindy
               Not bad.

                    Mark
               Sicko

                    Cindy
               Just sayin'.

Mark drags Cop 2 into the corner of the room against the wall.

                    Lucy
               You...gotta...get...outta...here.

                    Mark
               Why?

                    Lucy
               I'm dying!

Mark rushes over to Lucy.

                    Mark
          You're not. Hang in there kiddo. We're always bravest before the
                    storm and all.
                    Peter
               Let me at her.

                    Mark
               Lucky?

                    Peter
               It's the only way to end her suffering.

                    Mr. Tibbs
          I'd expect that kind of talk from her(points to Cindy).

                    Cindy
               Very funny.
               It may be the only way.

                    Cop 1
               (holding a table up against the window)
               Could I have a hand here?

The zombie wrestles free of the jacket.

                    Cop 1

Oh shit!

           Peter
         (to Cop 1)
      Gimme your gun!

          Cop 2
    I got it, don't worry.

          Peter
    Shoot it in the head!

Cop 2 shoots zombie in the head.

          Cop 2
      Told you.

          Mark
   We need more fire power!

          Cop 1
    Stop screaming.

The zombies, outside, stop attacking.

          Cop 2

     They stopped.

There are three knocks on the door.

          Mark
  Why would a zombie knock?

         Mr. Tibbs
      Open it.

          Mark
  What, and let those things in?

          Cop 1
      Okay.

Cop 1 opens the door, Cop 2 squinting at the light peeking it. A silhouette of a woman with dreads is in the foreground. She shakes a staff with beads and rattlesnake tails at them.

               Cindy
             Mother...

            Mr. Tibbs
            Mother??

Cindy shrugs and goes to the Voodoo Queen's side.

           Voodoo Queen
I laid a curse on this town that the wicked an power would fumble.
              John 4:16 "I shall return."

               Cindy
And he will with his army of undead soldiers to lay a curse on the
     world (pats her belly-looking at Tibbs) in your unborn son.

            Mr. Tibbs
            My unborn?

Tibbs drops to his knees.

              Mark
           We can fix this.

            Mr Tibbs.
            It's no use.

The zombies start converging on the room. Lucy comes to and grabs
Mark. Peter chops off her head, slicing it off but getting the knife
stuck in the bone. He pries it out and gives her head a good whack.
It falls to the side.

              Mark
              Lucy!

              Peter
      She was going to eat you like butterscotch.

              Mark
I'm not sure if I'm safer in here with you or out there with the
           zombies! C'mon Tibbs, get up!

            Mr. Tibbs
           Yeah...yeah...

               Cindy
Come stand at my side and we will reign over the world with your
                unborn heir.

> Mr. Tibbs
> No, never.

> Mark
> Tibbs, c'mon we gotta get outta here.

> Cop 1
> We have a panic room.

> Peter
> Is there room for four?

> Mark
> You ain't lockin' me up with him!

Interior: Jail cell. Cop 1 locks Peter up in the cell.

> Peter
> Aw, c'mon.

> Cop 1
> When they come for you, stay clear of the bars, you should be safe.

> Peter
> You fuckers!
> I saved your lives!

> Mr. Tibbs
> Sorry Pete.

> Cop 1
> C'mon! This way!

They run into a storm cellar and shut the door behind them.

> Mark
> You call this a panic room? Where are the lights?

> Cop 1
> (flicking them on)
> Over here.

> Mr. Tibbs
> Fuck that's bright.

> Cop 2
> Won't the light attract them?

> Cop 1

                         No, it's air-tight seals.

                                    Cop 2
                    Then there's no ventilation? How will we breathe?

                                    Cop 1
                    There are vents, here I forgot to turn them on.

                                  Mr. Tibbs
                                   Ok, good.

Interior: Storm cellar. They're sweating while sleeping on the floor.
Tibbs wakes up and shakes Mark awake.

                                   Mr Tibbs
                    It's fuckin' hot in here. The walls, they're hot.

Mark shakes Cop 1 awake.

                                    Mark
                             Hey, the walls are hot.

                                    Cop 1
                                 They're cement.

Exterior: Police station as seen from the outside is ablaze.

                                    Cop 1
                               Shit, you're right.

                                    Cop 2
                           They're burning the place down.

Interior: Peter is running around the police station with a torch,
lighting things ablaze.

                                    Peter
                         Forgot I had the key-fuckers!

Zombies are falling to the ground torched. Peter comes around back
and sees a pipe labelled "main line natural gas".

                                    Peter
                                    Hello.

Peter kickes the pipe until it bursts open, spewing gas.

                                    Peter
                         Say, "That's all, folks." Pigs.

Gas lines erupt through the town as it explodes into flames.

Exterior: Peter is maniacally laughing.

                Cindy
             It was you!

                Peter
             Me, what?

                Cindy
    The maniac killer. You're a man after my own heart.

                Peter
You have a heart in there (pointing to her belly). I can help raise
                that pup.

                Cindy
  This isn't a regular bun in the oven-I'm on a strict diet.

                Peter
   (breaking off a zombie's arm laying charred on the ground)
          I know-zombie extra crispy.

Cindy takes a big bite out of the arm and motions him to eat.

                Peter
         I like mine rare.

Interior: Storm cellar. Smoke starts to pour in through the
ventilation. The sound of the Voodoo Queen's rattling staff can be
heard with the pounding of a drum in the pace of a heartbeat.

            Voodoo Queen
             (chanting)

                Cop 2
       They're trying to smoke up out!

                Cop 1
             Shut up!

Cop 2 gurgles and chokes- blue comes out of his mouth.

                Mark
             Aw, shit!

              Mr. Tibbs

                        Shoot him!

                          Cop 1
                 I can't. He's my nephew.

                          Mark
In a couple of seconds it won't be your nephew anymore. I'd do it but
                   I've never fired a gun.

                          Cop 1
                Here. Just squeeze the trigger.

                          Mark
                       (hesitates)
                        I can't.

Tibbs picks up a 2x4 and proceeds to beat Cop 2 over the head
repeatedly.

                       Mr. Tibbs
         I'll be damned if I let a smokey eat my flesh.

Tibbs drops the plank of wood. They begin coughing. Tibbs hands them
blankets.

                       Mr. Tibbs
             Wrap yourselves in these. Open the door.
                          Mark
                      But the flames.

                       Mr. Tibbs.
           Stay here and roast then. I'll take my chances.

Cop 1 opens the door- flames erupt around them. They race down a
corridor. Through the crackling fire the sound of a baby crying is
heard.

                          Mark
                      What the fuck?

                          Cop 1
                       I don't know.

                          Mark
                       A baby here?

                          Cop 1
                   Look, you better hurry.

A cross beam busts loose from the ceiling and falls onto Cop 1. A zombie comes around the corner, ripping out Cop 1's intestines.

> Cop 1
> Keep moving!

Mark turns to Tibbs, but goes after the baby's crying. Tibbs pushes his way through the flames and out the front door, narrowly escaping.

Interior: Mark is standing next to the jail cell.

> Mark
> Kid, where are you?

Peter comes out from behind a corner, making the sound of a crying baby.

> Mark
> Lucky?

> Peter
> I told you, I'm not your lucky charm.

> Mark
> Peter, stop!

Peter drives the knife into Mark, lifting him off the ground. Peter twists the knife.

> Peter
> Much better dead!

It rips out the umbilical cord. The Voodoo Queen's chanting is now frenetic. The demon child chews off its umbilical cord and moves toward Tibbs, its mouth gaping open. Tibbs backs up slowly, tripping tripping over a rock and falling. He gets up, picking up the rock and holding it high above the infant's head

The infant looks at him innocently.

Tibbs lowers the rock and drops it to his side.

The infant smirks, then lunges at Tibbs.

Tibbs yanks him off.

Peter emerges from the darkness.

          PETER
Had second thoughts about killing your offspring?

          MR. TIBBS
The second coming...

          PETER
And the flesh of the dead made Lord.

          VOODOO QUEEN
Back away from the child.

          PETER
I swore to Cindy I'd raise him! You can't...

          VOODOO QUEEN
I can.

          MR. TIBBS
This has to end.

          VOODOO QUEEN
It is only the beginning of the end.

Zombies begin to surround Tibbs.

          MR. TIBBS
         (shoving them off)
No!

Peter looks at Tibbs- then the child- then at the knife in his bloody hand and slits the throat of the infant.

A large propane tank explodes behind them, killing several zombies. Tibbs sees another tank ready to explode.

Peter looks at his knife, again.

          PETER
The thrill kill. Shrill with the shriek of mine own.

He drops to his knees and guts himself, laughing, teary eyed.

          VOODOO QUEEN

                        The child!

The tank erupts, sending Tibbs hurtling into the air, he lands on a
dusty stretch of road.

Exterior: Sunrise. The charred remains of the town are in the
distance as Tibbs awakes. He limps through what's left of the town.
He finds his guitar sitting on the remains of his Chevy.

                        Mr. Tibbs
                          Huh!

He strums a chord and walks into the sunrise.

Exterior: Swamp. The Voodoo Queen sets down the corpse of the infant
demon child wrapped in a blanket, and begins to chant with her head
bowed,

TELOS?

www.ingramcontent.com/pod-product-compliance
Lightning Source LLC
Chambersburg PA
CBHW081752170526
45167CB00009B/4007